孔子学院总部／
国家汉办汉语国际推广成都基地规划教材

走进天府系列教材【成都印象】

# 品川茶

### Let's Drink Sichuan Tea

西 南 财 经 大 学
汉语国际推广成都基地　著

西南财经大学出版社
中国·成都

西南财经大学
汉语国际推广成都基地 著

**总策划** 涂文涛

**策　划**

李永强

**主　编**

梁　婷　白巧燕

**编　者**

《成都印象·游成都》　胡倩琳

《成都印象·居成都》　郑　莹

《成都印象·吃川菜》　谢　娟　王　新

《成都印象·品川茶》　肖　静

《成都印象·饮川酒》　谢　娟

《成都印象·看川剧》　郑　莹

《成都印象·绣蜀绣》　谢　娟

《成都印象·梦三国之蜀国》　蒋林益　胡佩迦

《成都印象·悟道教》　沙　莎　吕　彦　陈　茉

《成都印象·练武术》　邓　帆　刘　亚

**审　订** 冯卫东

**英文翻译**

Alexander Demmelhuber

# Introduction

*Let's Drink Sichuan Tea* is one part of the "Impressions of Chengdu" textbook series, which is promoted by the Chengdu Base of Confucius Institute Headquarters and published by the Southwestern University of Finance and Economics. This book contains 7 units, which are designed on the basis of the Confucius Institute Headquarters'/Hanban's "International Curriculum for Chinese Language Education" (hereinafter referred to as "Curriculum"), as can be seen, for example, on vocabulary and language points used, and ensures that this textbook is held to scientific, systematic and rigorous standards.

This book mainly introduces Sichuan tea, Chengdu's gaiwan tea culture, teahouse culture, the famous tea-horse trade as well as the Belt and Road Initiative, which carries on the spirit of the tea-horse trade on the Silk Road. The lessons strive to be as practical as possible, vivid and colorful, and aim to help international students of Chinese learn about and understand Sichuan tea culture through language and background information.

This book is mainly composed of vocabulary and grammar items as can be found in the Curriculum for levels 3 to 5, with some everyday Chinese expressions mixed in. We hope that this book will help beginner and intermediate students of Chinese to lay a solid foundation for their Chinese and comprehensively improve their proficiency, as well as adding to their knowledge about Sichuan tea culture.

Hopefully, you will enjoy *Let's Drink Sichuan Tea* and we are looking forward to any criticism or suggestions you might have. Hanban gave us much help and support during editing of this book and we would like to take this opportunity to express our gratitude.

## 前　言

　　《品川茶》是西南财经大学汉语国际推广成都基地推出的《成都印象》系列教材之一。全书共7课，以孔子学院总部/国家汉办的《国际汉语教学通用课程大纲》为基本编写依据，涉及大纲中的大量词汇、语言点等指标，以保证教材的科学性、系统性和严谨性。

　　本书集中介绍了四川茶叶、成都盖碗茶文化、茶馆文化、历史上有名的茶马互市以及茶马互市中体现的丝路精神、"一带一路"等内容，力求贴近生活，生动有趣，为外国汉语学习者了解及学习四川茶文化提供语言和信息的支持。

　　本书语料以《大纲》中的3-5级词汇和语法项目为主，加入了一些生活中的常用汉语，希望能帮助初中级水平汉语学习者打下扎实的基础，全面提升汉语水平，并且丰富他们关于四川茶文化的知识。

　　希望您能喜欢《品川茶》这本教材，也希望您对本书提出批评和建议。本书的编写得到了国家汉办的大力支持和帮助，在此一并表示感谢。

目录

**第一课**
Lesson 1
[ 川茶简介 ]
[ Introduction of Sichuan Tea ]
01 - 08

**第二课**
Lesson 2
[ 成都盖碗茶 ]
[ Chengdu's Gaiwan Tea ]
09 - 16

**第三课**
Lesson 3
[ 四川名茶 ]
[ Sichuan's Famous Teas ]
17 - 27

**第四课**
Lesson 4
[ 成都茶馆 ]
[ Chengdu's Teahouses ]
28 - 41

第五课　〔茶马互市〕　　42 - 50
Lesson 5　〔 The Tea-Horse Trade 〕

第六课　〔川茶与"一带一路"〕　　51 - 59
Lesson 6　〔 Sichuan Tea and "The Belt and Road" 〕

第七课　〔古今川茶〕　　60 - 62
Lesson 7　〔 Ancient and Modern Sichuan Tea 〕

〔参考文献〕　　63
〔 References 〕

# 第一课 〔川茶简介〕
## Lesson 1 〔 Introduction of Sichuan Tea 〕

① 发源地　　fāyuándì
② 悠 久　　　yōujiǔ
③ 种 植　　　zhòngzhí
④ 产 量　　　chǎnliàng
⑤ 居……之首　jū…zhīshǒu
⑥ 宠 儿　　　chǒngér
⑦ 设 备　　　shèbèi
⑧ 休 闲　　　xiūxián
⑨ 娱 乐　　　yúlè
⑩ 去 处　　　qùchù

　　四川被称为中国茶文化的发源地。川茶历史悠久，已有三千多年的种植历史，早在两千多年前就已经成为重要的商品，在唐宋时期，川茶产量居当时全国之首。同时，川茶品种繁多，其中著名的有蒙顶甘露、竹叶青、峨眉雪芽等，都是国内外爱茶一族的宠儿。

　　值得一提的还有成都的茶馆，它可是川茶文化的一大特点。成都的茶馆发展快，数量多，设备也很齐全，是休闲娱乐的好去处。在茶馆里不仅可以喝茶，还可以摆龙门阵（聊天）、谈生意、招待客人、打牌娱乐等等。

　　好了，是不是很想喝喝川茶呢？那就跟大萌和大萌的朋友们一起去茶馆逛逛吧……

（一）今天一起去喝茶吧！

（大萌、文小西、江一华躺在西南财大草坪上晒着太阳聊天）

大 萌：
　　坐，请坐，请上座。茶，上茶，上好茶。

**文**小西：

上茶是什么茶？好喝吗？

**江**一华：

看来你还不太了解中国茶，上茶是把茶端上来请人喝的意思……

**大**萌：

一华说得对！中国人常说："早晨开门七件事，柴米油盐酱醋茶。"可见，茶是中国人生活中的必需品呢。走，去喝茶吧！我们一起好好了解一下川茶！

**文**小西：

太好了！咱们要坐上座，喝好茶！

## （二）川茶有3 000多岁了！

**江**一华：

川茶是中国最早的茶叶吗？

**大**萌：

没错，川茶有3 000多岁了！在中国，种茶、饮茶最早的地方就是四川。

① 温 馨　wēnxīn
② 端　　duān
③ 建 筑　jiànzhù
④ 恢 复　huīfù
⑤ 修 建　xiūjiàn
⑥ 参 照　cānzhào
⑦ 欣 赏　xīnshǎng
⑧ 民 俗　mínsú
⑨ 眼见为实　yǎn jiàn wéi shí
⑩ 体 会　tǐhuì
⑪ 魅 力　mèilì

文小西：
　这里有家茶馆，我们进去尝尝吧。

江一华：
　顺兴老茶馆看上去像明清建筑，它有多少年的历史了？

大　萌：
　这家顺兴老茶馆是 1999 年恢复修建的，是中国最大的一家茶馆。它参照了成都从古代到现代的著名茶馆、茶楼的特点，可以说是东方民族特色的茶文化历史博物馆。

江一华：
　中外同赏戏，古今皆品茶。在这里大家可以边品茶边赏戏，还可以欣赏墙壁上的精美图案。

大　萌：
　顺兴老茶馆有四大特点——喝盖碗茶、尝成都名小吃、看川剧、观民俗与了解成都历史，处处都能看到特别的巴蜀茶文化。

文小西：
　眼见为实。我们快进去体会一下这座老茶馆的魅力吧。

(Panda Da Meng is taking you to Chengdu's teahouses! Let's stroll around the teahouses with Da Meng and have some fragrant Sichuan tea.)

Sichuan is called the place of origin of China's tea culture. Sichuan tea has a long history: plants have been cultivated for more than three thousand years and tea became an important commodity as early as two thousand years ago. During the Tang and Song Dynasties, they were a big cultural highlight. There are many of them, they expand fast and they boast a wide range of equipment. They are good places for leisure and entertainment. Teahouses are not only places for drinking tea, but also for, e.g., chatting, discussing business, entertaining guests, playing cards and mahjong as well as other recreational activities.

All right! You should be all eager about having some Sichuan tea now, right? Then let's go on a stroll around the teahouses with Da Meng and his friends!

Part 1  Let's Have Some Tea Together Today!

(Da Meng / Wen Xiaoxi / Jiang Yihua are lying on the lawn basking in the sun, chatting)

**Da Meng:** Have a seat and some good tea.

**Wen Xiaoxi:** What is "shang" tea? Is it good?

**Jiang Yihua:** Looks like you're still not all that familiar with Chinese tea. "Shang cha" means placing the tea down and inviting the guests to drink .

**Da Meng:** Yihua is right! The Chinese like to say, "Firewood, rice, oil,salt, sauce, vinegar and tea are the seven necessities to begin a day". As you can see, tea is a necessity in Chinese people's lives. Let's go and have some tea! Let's get to know Sichuan tea together!

**Wen Xiaoxi/Jiang Yihua:** Wonderful! Let's sit down and have some good tea!

Part 2    Sichuan Tea Is Over 3,000 Years Old!

**Jiang Yihua:** Is Sichuan tea China's oldest tea?

**Da Meng:** It is. It is over 3,000 years old! The first people to cultivate and drink tea in China were the Sichuanese.

**Wen Xiaoxi:** There is a teahouse. Let's go inside and have some tea.

**Jiang Yihua:** The Shunxing Old Teahouse looks like a building from the Ming and Qing Dynasties. How old is it?

**Da Meng:** This teahouse was restored and built in 1999; it is China's biggest teahouse. Its characteristics consult that of the most famous Chengdu teahouses from antiquity until modernity. You could say it is an Asian tea culture museum.

**Jiang Yihua:** People from near and afar enjoy theater; from ancient times until today, people drink tea. Here, everybody can enjoy theater over a cup of tea. You can also appreciate the beautiful motifs on the wall.

**Da Meng:** The Shunxing Old Teahouse has four features you can enjoy: gaiwan tea, Chengdu's famous snacks, Sichuan opera, folk customs as well as Chengdu's history. The place oozes Sichuan tea culture.

**Wen Xiaoxi:** Seeing is believing. Let's get inside and experience this teahouse's charm for ourselves.

# 词语

| | |
|---|---|
| 柴 | 油 |
| 柴 chái<br>firewood | 油 yóu<br>oil |

| | | | |
|---|---|---|---|
| qīng xiāng pū bí<br>清香扑鼻 | fragrant | chǒng ér<br>宠儿 | favourite |
| chǎn liàng<br>产量 | output | chái<br>柴 | firewood |
| zhòng zhí<br>种植 | plant | jū … zhī shǒu<br>居……之首 | rank first |
| yōu jiǔ<br>悠久 | long | xiū xián<br>休闲 | have leisure |
| shè bèi<br>设备 | equipment | yú lè<br>娱乐 | entertain |

| fā yuán dì 发 源 地 | place of origin |
|---|---|
| qù chù 去 处 | place |
| wēn xīn 温 馨 | soft and sweet; warm |
| jiàng 酱 | soy sauce |
| huī fù 恢 复 | renew; restore |
| xīn shǎng 欣 赏 | appreciate |
| mín sú 民 俗 | folk custom |
| mèi lì 魅 力 | glamour; charm |

| duān 端 | hold sth. level with both hands; carry |
|---|---|
| dǎ pái 打 牌 | play mahjong or cards |
| yán 盐 | salt |
| jiàn zhù 建 筑 | building |
| xiū jiàn 修 建 | build; construct |
| cān zhào 参 照 | consult and follow |
| tǐ huì 体 会 | know or learn from experience; realize |
| cù 醋 | vinegar |

## 语言点

1. 不仅……还 / 而且
2. 还
3. 反问句

## 思考

1. "上茶"是什么意思?
2. 茶对中国人来说重要吗?
3. 川茶有多少年的历史了?
4. 顺兴老茶馆有什么特点?
5. 你去过茶馆吗? 说一说你的经历。

[ 成都盖碗茶 ]

[ Chengdu's Gaiwan Tea ]

## （一）绿茶、红茶还是茉莉花茶?

① 正 宗 zhèngzōng
② 冲　　 chōng

**文小西:**

这么多茶叶! 蒙顶黄芽、蒙顶甘露、峨眉竹叶青、碧潭飘雪、工夫红茶, 它们有什么不同呢?

**大 萌:**

我喜欢茉莉花茶, 打算来一杯碧潭飘雪, 你们喜欢绿茶的话就点竹叶青或者蒙顶甘露, 喜欢红茶可以试试川红, 都挺不错的。

**文小西:**

盖碗茶是正宗的川味, 我来一杯。

**江一华:**

我也来一杯!

**大 萌:**

好, 先点茶叶, 然后再让他们表演冲盖碗茶。

## （二）成都盖碗茶来了

**文** 小西：

快看！那位师傅一手拿黄色的茶壶，一手拿了很多白色的碗和银色的碟子，看起来挺重的！

**大** 萌：

黄色的是铜茶壶，银色的是锡杯托，茶艺师为了方便和速度快，一只手要拿一二十套茶具呢，确实很重。

**江** 一华：

盖碗茶的表演太精彩了！我们快喝茶吧！

**大** 萌：

不着急，等5分钟再喝，茶更香。喝盖碗茶的时候分五步——净具、置茶、沏茶、闻香、品饮，这样喝茶才有风情。

**文** 小西：

咦，那个人已经走了，为什么还把茶盖放在椅子上？太没礼貌了吧。

**大** 萌：

他马上就回来。

① 净 具　jìngjù
② 置 茶　zhìchá
③ 沏 茶　qīchá
④ 闻 香　wénxiāng
⑤ 品 饮　pǐnyǐn
⑥ 恶作剧　èzuòjù
⑦ 暗 号　ànhào
⑧ 加 水　jiāshuǐ
⑨ 扣　　　kòu

文小西：

　　他一定是忘了，是恶作剧吧。

江一华：

　　你看，这么多人等着喝茶，可是大家都不去坐他的位子。

大　萌：

　　看！那个人回来了。告诉你们吧，这茶盖是"暗号"哦。茶盖放桌上，是说没茶了，让服务员快来加水；茶盖扣在竹椅上，意思是这个位子有人了，一会儿就回来。

文小西：

　　真有意思，我也来试试。

盖碗茶是成都茶馆的一个特色，喝盖碗茶能感受到地地道道的川味。说起成都茶馆，人们首先想到的就是"盖碗茶"。盖碗茶的茶具是由茶碗、茶盖、茶船组合而成。这三件套的意思是"天盖之（茶盖），地载之（茶船），人育之（茶碗）"。盖碗茶的独特之处在于茶船，它是一千多年前一位女子在成都发明的，最开始是为了防止烫手，一直延续至今。

成都的盖碗茶，从茶具到服务都非常特别。用铜茶壶、锡杯托、白瓷碗泡成的茶，色香味形俱全，喝后也会感觉香甜，而且茶客还可以看到泡茶的绝技。

① 延 续 yánxù
② 铜 tóng
③ 锡 xī
④ 瓷 cí
⑤ 绝 技 juéjì

Part 1　Green Tea, Black Tea or Jasmine Tea?

(Inside the Shunxing Old Teahouse)

**Wen Xiaoxi:** So many teas! Mengding Huangya, Mengding Ganlu, Emei Zhuye Qing, Bitan Piaoxue and Congou. What's their difference?

**Jiang Yihua:** I have no idea either. I know only about green tea and black tea. Da Meng, please tell us more.

**Da Meng:** I like jasmine tea, so I'm going with a cup of Bitan Piaoxue. If you like green tea, you can order Zhuye Qing or Mengding Ganlu. If black tea is more to your liking, you can try Chuanhong. You can't go wrong either way.

**Wen Xiaoxi:** Gaiwan tea carries that authentic Sichuan flavor. I'll take one cup.

**Jiang Yihua:** Same here!

**Da Meng:** All right. Let's order the tea first and then watch the waiter pour boiling water onto the tea, which is quite the spectacle.

Part 2   There It Is: Chengdu Gaiwan Tea!

**Wen Xiaoxi:** Look! He has the yellow teapot in one hand, and a lot of white cups and silver saucers in the other hand. They look so heavy!

**Da Meng:** The yellow one is the copper tea kettle and the silver ones are the tin saucers. The tea master holds ten to twenty tea sets in one hand for convenience's and speed's sakes. They are indeed heavy.

**Jiang Yihua:** What a brilliant performance! Let's have some tea!

**Da Meng:** Don't get excited. Wait five minutes until you drink; the tea will be even more fragrant then. There are five steps to drinking gaiwan tea, namely cleaning the cup, putting tea into the cup, pouring boiling water into the cup, smelling the fragrant flavor, sampling and drinking the tea. Only then is there grace to tea drinking.

**Wen Xiaoxi:** Hey, he already left. Why did he leave the lid on the chair? How rude!

**Da Meng:** He'll be back right away.

**Wen Xiaoxi:** He forgot for sure. This is definitely a prank.

**Jiang Yihua:** Look, there are so many people waiting to drink tea, but nobody's taking his place.

**Da Meng:** Look! He's back. I'll let you onto something: this lid is a secret signal. If the lid is placed on the table, it means there's no more tea, which leads the waiter to pour more water into the cup. Placing the lid upside down on a bamboo chair means that this seat is already occupied and the person in question will return shortly.

**Wen Xiaoxi:** Fascinating! I also want to give it a try.

Gaiwan tea is one of Chengdu's teahouses' specialties and carries that authentic Sichuan flavor. Speaking of Chengdu teahouses, the first thing that comes to mind is "Gaiwan tea". The Gaiwan tea set consists of a cup, a lid and a saucer. These three parts stand for: heaven (lid), earth (saucer) and people (cup). The gaiwan's most prominent feature is the saucer, which was invented over one thousand years ago by a woman in Chengdu. It was invented to prevent the tea drinker's hand from getting scalded and it continues to fulfill this role until today.

Chengdu's gaiwan tea is special in every way, from its tea set to its service. The tea is brewed in a copper kettle, served in a white porcelain cup on top of a tin saucer and tea smells, looks and tastes great, and has a sweet aftertaste. Teahouse guests may also appreciate the tea ceremony, a special performance of its own.

词 语

| 沏 茶 | qīchá infuse(with boiling water) |

| 闻 香 | wénxiāng smell the fragrant flavor of tea |

| zhèng zōng 正 宗 | authentic |
| zhì chá 置 茶 | put tea into the cup |
| àn hào 暗 号 | a secret signal; countersign |
| dié zi 碟 子 | small plate |
| pǐn yǐn 品 饮 | sample tea and drink tea |

| jiā shuǐ 加 水 | add more water |
| chōng 冲 | pour boiling water on |
| è zuò jù 恶 作 剧 | a practical joke |
| kòu 扣 | place a cup, bowl etc. upside down |
| yán xù 延 续 | continue |

| | |
|---|---|
| cí<br>瓷 | porcelain |
| tóng<br>铜 | copper |

| | |
|---|---|
| jué jì<br>绝 技 | stunt |
| xī<br>锡 | tin |

| | |
|---|---|
| jìng jù<br>净 具 | make cups clean |

# 语言点

1. 离合词：上茶、品茶、净具、置茶、沏茶、闻香、品饮
2. 为了

# 思考

1. 什么叫作盖碗茶？

2. 成都盖碗茶是谁发明的？

3. 顺兴老茶馆有没有盖碗茶的表演？

4. 摆放茶盖是什么"暗号"？

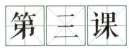 〔四川名茶〕

Lesson 3 〔 Sichuan's Famous Teas 〕

① 三炒三揉  sānchǎo sānróu
② 开 端  kāiduān
③ 献 茶  xiànchá
④ 茶 道  chádào

## （一）这么多种川茶

江一华：
今天喝的绿茶甘甜美味，你的红茶怎么样？

文小西：
红茶也不错，我都快醉了。

大 萌：
川茶的品种很多，光有名的绿茶就有 32 种。

江一华：
还有哪些有名的川茶呢？

大 萌：
唐代著名诗人白居易在《琴茶》中写道："琴里知闻唯渌水，茶中故旧是蒙山"。蒙顶甘露是中国最古老的名茶，被尊为茶中故旧。

文小西：
峨眉竹叶青也很受欢迎。

## （二）蒙山顶上茶

**大萌：**

"扬子江心水，蒙山顶上茶。"我有一个梦想，用扬子江的水泡蒙山顶的茶，味道一定好极了！

**文小西：**

今天可是采茶、制茶一日游，我们好好享受一下蒙顶茶吧。

**江一华：**

我最想了解"三炒三揉"的传统制茶方法。

**大萌：**

蒙顶甘露是历史名茶，不仅茶好，茶文化更是丰富多彩。蒙顶山茶技、茶道、茶艺都有上千年历史，是中国茶道的开端。

**江一华：**

我们去看看茶技表演，怎么样？

**大萌：**

好，蒙顶茶技"龙行十八式"非常有名，就是十八种献茶的技艺。

**文小西：**

那我可要学两招。

① 修身养性　xiūshēn yǎngxìng
② 美心修德　měixīn xiūdé
③ 核　心　　héxīn
④ 领　会　　lǐnghuì

江一华：

　　他们每一个表演的动作都像龙一样，同时正好把茶倒进盖碗里。

文小西：

　　真是太神奇、太帅了！

江一华：

　　我常听中国人说茶道精神，这是什么意思？

大　萌：

　　茶道就是把茶饮作为一种修身养性之道（方法、精神），通过沏茶、赏茶、闻茶、饮茶，增进友谊，美心修德。

江一华：

　　茶道是什么时候开始的？

大　萌：

　　茶道最早起源于中国。中国的茶道在隋朝之前开始慢慢发展，形成于唐代，宋明时期最为繁荣。《茶经》的作者陆羽创立了中国茶道。茶道是茶文化的核心。中国茶道不仅重视饮茶艺能（茶艺），还重视饮茶时的自然环境、人际关系和茶人的心态；它体现了中国古代哲学思想。

**江一华：**

看来我还需要好好领会一番呢。

①施 主　shīzhǔ
②香 客　xiāngkè
③云 游　yúnyóu

## （三）峨眉山的茶叶

**文小西：**

峨眉山真美，不但寺庙多，茶叶也挺多的。

**大 萌：**

峨眉山的绿茶很有名，比如峨眉雪芽、竹叶青等。

**江一华：**

庙里有茶园，生产佛茶——峨眉雪芽。

**大 萌：**

峨眉山的宗教茶文化有 3 000 多年历史了，峨眉山的道家和佛门产的茶叶不是用来交易的，而是送给施主、香客喝的，如果有云游僧人来，峨眉雪芽就是上好的礼物了。

**文小西：**

喝了这么多茶叶，今天终于可以换换口味，喝竹叶了，不过怎么还是茶叶的味道呢？

**大 萌：**

这就是茶叶，因为看起来像竹叶，所以叫竹叶青。

**江一华：**

泡竹叶青常常用玻璃杯，这有什么讲究吗？

大 萌:

除了喝竹叶青盖碗茶以外，更多人喜欢用透明玻璃杯，可以欣赏绿色的茶叶在水中的样子和那种清亮的感觉。

江一华:

峨眉山的景美，茶美，人更美呀！

Part 1　So Many Sichuan Teas!

**Jiang Yihua:** This green tea is fragrant and sweet. What about your black tea?

**Wen Xiaoxi:** The black tea is really good. I'm about to…

**Da Meng:** There are lots of different Sichuan teas. There are 32 different famous green teas alone.

**Jiang Yihua:** What are the other famous Sichuan teas?

**Da Meng:** Famous Tang poet Bai Juyi wrote in his poem *Qin and Tea*, "Of tunes, the qin knows only old Green Water; of tea, the herb's most ageless leaf is Mt. Meng's". Mengding Ganlu is China's oldest famous tea and revered as ageless.

**Wen Xiaoxi:** Emei Zhunye Qing tea is also very popular.

Part 2　Having Tea on Mt. Mengding

**Da Meng:** "Water of Yangtze River and tea of the peak of Mt. Meng". My dream is to use water from the Yangtze and make tea from the top of Mt. Meng, the taste would definitely be something else!

**Wen Xiaoxi:** Today we're on a day trip for picking and producing tea, though. Let's enjoy some good Mengding tea.

**Jiang Yihua:** I want to know more about the traditional method of producing tea.

**Da Meng:** Mengding Ganlu is a famous tea with a long history. Not only is the tea itself a delight, its culture is rich and varied. Mengding's tea skills, tea ceremony and tea art have a history of more than one thousand years. The tea ceremony started in Mengding.

**Jiang Yihua:** Let's go watch a performance of these tea skills, how about it?

**Da Meng:** Sure. The"Eighteen Movements of the Flying Dragon" is a famous Mengding tea skill and describes 18 skills of presenting tea.

**Wen Xiaoxi:** I also want to learn some!

**Jiang Yihua:** The performers' every movement are just like that of a dragon while they put the tea into the gaiwan.

**Wen Xiaoxi:** Wow, that sounds so cool!

**Jiang Yihua:** I often hear Chinese talk about this"tea ceremony". What is that about?

**Da Meng:** The Way of Tea treats drinking tea as a way of cultivating one's moral character and nourishing one's nature. Through steeping, appreciating, smelling and drinking the tea, friendships deepen and one may enrich their minds and cultivate their moral characters.

**Jiang Yihua:** When did this tea ceremony start?

**Da Meng:** The tea ceremony started in China. China's tea ceremony slowly began to make its appearance during the Sui Dynasty, took shape in the Tang Dynasty and was at its peak during the Song and Ming Dynasties. *The Classic of Tea*'s author Lu Yu created the tea ceremony. The ceremony is at the core of tea culture. China's tea ceremony not only attaches great importance to the mastery of drinking tea, but also to the surroundings while drinking tea, to interpersonal relationships and to the tea drinker's state of mind. The ceremony embodied ancient China's philosophical thinking.

**Jiang Yihua:** Looks like there's much to learn for me.

Part 3  Mt. Emei's Tea

**Wen Xiaoxi:** Emei is so stunning! There are lots of temples and also quite a lot of teas.

**Da Meng:** Emei's green teas, like Emei Xueya and Zhuye Qing, are famous.

**Jiang Yihua:** There is a tea garden in the temple; they are producing Fo tea here – and also Emei Xueya.

**Da Meng:** Mt. Emei's religious tea culture has a history of more than 3,000 years. The tea produced by Daoists and Buddhists is not for trade, but is gifted to patrons and pilgrims. For wandering monks, Emei Xueya also makes a good gift.

**Wen Xiaoxi:** We had so much tea already; I'm glad we can finally taste some new flavors. I just had some bamboo tea. How come it still tastes like tea?

**Da Meng:** These are still tea leaves. They look like bamboo leaves. That's why they're called Zhuye Qing.

**Jiang Yihua:** You often see people using glass cups for making Zhuye Qing. Is there more to that?

**Da Meng:** Some enjoy drinking Zhuye Qing tea in a gaiwan, but even more prefer transparent glass cups, so they can enjoy a crystal-clear view of the green tea leaves in the water.

**Jiang Yihua:**Mt. Emei's scenery is beautiful and so is its tea, but its people are even more so.

## 词 语

| 核 心 | héxīn<br>core; kernel | 云 游 | yúnyóu<br>(of a Buddhist<br>monk) wander about | 香 客 | xiāngkè<br>a worshipper at a<br>Buddhist temple |
|---|---|---|---|---|---|

| sān chǎo sān róu<br>三 炒 三 揉 | working procedure of making tea | kāi duān<br>开 端 | start; beginning |
|---|---|---|---|
| xiàn chá<br>献 茶 | present tea | chá dào<br>茶 道 | tea ceremony |
| xiū shēn yǎng xìng<br>修 身 养 性 | cultivate one's moral character and nourish one's nature | lǐng huì<br>领 会 | understand |
| shī zhǔ<br>施 主 | (monks', or nuns', formal address for a layman)patron | měi xīn xiū dé<br>美 心 修 德 | prettify one's mind and cultivate one's moral character |

## 语言点

1. 光

2. 被

3. v+ 于：起源于；形成于

4. 不是……而是……

## 思 考

1. 四川有哪些有名的茶叶？

2. 蒙顶茶是什么茶？蒙顶茶技又是什么？

3. 怎么理解茶道？

4. 峨眉茶有哪些？

5. 峨眉山的茶文化有什么不同？

# 第四课 〔成都茶馆〕
# Lesson 4 〔Chengdu's Teahouses〕

## （一）摆龙门阵

**江一华：**

　　我常听成都人说"摆龙门阵"，是什么意思？

**大 萌：**

　　哈哈，我们现在就在"摆龙门阵"，就是聊天的意思。

**文小西：**

　　我们还去上次的茶馆"摆龙门阵"吧，边喝茶边摆。

**大 萌：**

　　好，茶馆是摆龙门阵的好地方。

**江一华：**

　　有时候咖啡馆太安静了，说话不能大声，还是茶馆好。

**大 萌：**

　　没错，茶馆不论刮风下雨，全天开放；茶客中有各行各业的人，奇闻逸事自然也多，聊起来有趣极了。成都人说"龙门阵打伙摆，茶钱各给各"，意思是不认识的人聊起来也自在，这可是真正的成都茶馆文化。

① 奇闻逸事　qíwén yìshì
② 惬 意　qièyì
③ 市 井　shìjǐng
④ 谈笑风生　tánxiào fēngshēng

江一华：

成都的茶馆不计其数，除了顺兴老茶馆以外，还有哪些有名的茶馆呢？

大　萌：

成都最平民的老茶馆要数人民公园的鹤鸣茶馆了，人均三十块钱，泡杯碧潭飘雪的盖碗茶可以坐上大半天，因为是露天茶馆，客人可以坐在树荫下、小湖边，很惬意。类似的还有文殊院的露天茶座、百花潭公园的露天茶座、府南河边的岁月茶庄。最有历史感和市井感的是彭镇老茶馆，很多摄影爱好者都去那里采风，那里是当地老人的天下，每逢赶集，茶馆人山人海，人们一边品茶，一边海阔天空，谈笑风生，热闹极了。

江一华：

　　我也很感兴趣，咱们现在就出发吧。

文小西：

　　哇！这么多有味道的茶馆，我要全部逛一遍。

① 文艺范儿　wényìfànr
② 欣 慰　xīnwèi
③ 团 购　tuángòu
④ 实 惠　shíhuì
⑤ 功 效　gōngxiào
⑥ 养 生　yǎngshēng

## （二）茶馆表演

江一华：

　　大萌，爸爸妈妈要来中国看我，他们已经参观过成都的很多名胜古迹了，这次我带他们去哪儿好呢？

大 萌：

　　去茶馆怎么样？找一个环境好的茶馆，喝喝茶，聊聊天，吃吃成都小吃，还可以打打麻将呢。

文小西：

　　好主意。茶馆是成都人聊天、会客、谈生意、找工作、打麻将的好去处。

江一华：

　　好，这次让他们好好体验一下老成都的茶馆文化。

**大萌：**

茶馆的选择也比较多——以戏曲表演为特色的茶馆，比如"顺兴老茶馆"；以茶艺表演为主的茶馆，比如春熙路的"山中老茶馆"；还有现在年轻人很推崇的文艺范儿茶馆，比如"和境茶社""不远树下的院子"。

**江一华：**

我和爸妈先去"顺兴老茶馆"感受一下川剧、品尝一下四川小吃吧，那里的服务也很好。如果有时间，再去茶艺馆欣赏工夫茶的表演。

（文小西、大萌、江一华和江一华的父母在茶馆）

**服务员：**

今天这里有川剧表演，欢迎大家来观看。

**江一华：**

这家茶馆的川剧表演非常受欢迎。爸、妈等会我们一起看吧。

**爸妈：**

好的，一华，你的汉语进步挺大的。

**文小西：**

一华一来成都就爱上了这里，他在很努力地学习中文和中国文化呢。

**爸** 爸：

那太好了！我回去告诉奶奶，她一定很欣慰。

**大** 萌：

大家快坐下来喝茶吧，一华，你来给大家介绍介绍川茶，你现在也算是专家啦。

**江** 一华：

爸爸，你爱喝绿茶，就喝竹叶青吧。妈妈，你试试花茶。

**爸** 妈：

好，好！

**大** 萌：

哇！快看！川剧变脸开始了！

## （三）茶艺馆

**文** 小西：

我们逛了快两个小时了，有点累，去喝点工夫茶，休息一下，怎么样？

**江** 一华：

好主意，这里有团购工夫茶，环境好，价格又实惠，就在这儿歇歇吧。

文小西：

这茶的味道清香，不过服务员把第一杯茶倒了，是不是有点浪费，那可都是精华！

大萌：

第一杯茶是不能喝的，这叫洗茶，是工夫茶里特有的程序。

文小西：

好吧！我还有个问题，这么多茶叶，其实味道差别不大，到底有什么不同呢？

大萌：

茶叶的种类很多，有红茶，绿茶，青茶，功效都不太一样。红茶可以帮助消化，解除疲劳，调节肠胃，比如川红；绿茶可以防止衰老，降低血脂，比如竹叶青；青茶是有名的健美茶和美容茶，比如乌龙茶。

文小西：

这么神奇，那我要多喝川茶，好好养生、美容。

在四川，茶馆处处可见。统计显示，目前成都的茶馆或茶楼有 3 万多家，有环境高雅的，也有朴素的、传统的，各式各样，满足不同茶客的需要。四川茶馆起源之早、发展之快、设备之齐全、数量之多、功能之广，在全国数一数二。来到四川，来到成都，如果不走进茶馆喝杯盖碗茶，那应该算是一个遗憾吧。在这里，喝茶不是为了解渴，更多的是享受休闲的时光。

早些时候，成都街边的大小茶馆，从早到晚客人满座，人们一坐少则两三个小时，多则一天。时光匆匆，这么多年过去了，成都闲适的生活就这样一代一代流传下来。

成都茶馆的功能是多方面的。首先，茶馆是摆龙门阵的最佳场所。这是因为：一是茶馆开得早、关得晚、有茶、有座，不论刮风下雨，全天开放，给摆龙门阵提供了舒适的环境；二是茶客来自四面八方，各行各业，他们带着自己的经历到茶馆，众多信息在茶馆汇集，又由茶客们带出去讲给别人听。"龙门阵"使茶馆越来越兴旺。其次，茶馆还有作为生意人的信息场的功能。做生意信息很重要，几个同行业的生意人约好去茶馆，一边喝茶，一边聊聊生意的事，有什么新消息大家一起分享。再次，茶馆也是朋友聚会的好地方，或热闹，或安静，茶客可以自由选择。最后，茶馆也是"大众俱乐部"。人们在茶馆可以观看川剧表演、下棋、打麻将、看书看报等。

① 高雅　　gāoyǎ
② 朴素　　pǔsù
③ 数一数二　shǔyī-shǔ'èr
④ 遗憾　　yíhàn
⑤ 闲适　　xiánshì
⑥ 匆匆　　cōngcōng

Part 1  Chatting

**Jiang Yihua:** I often hear people in Chengdu say "bǎi lóngménzhèn", what does it mean?

**Da Meng:** Haha, we're "bǎi lóngménzhèn" right now, it means chatting.

**Wen Xiaoxi:** Last time at the house we were also "bǎi lóngménzhèn", chatting over a cup of tea.

**Da Meng:** Right, teahouses are the perfect place for chatting.

**Jiang Yihua:** Cafés are sometimes way too quiet; you're not allowed to raise your voice and they have nothing on teahouses.

**Da Meng:** Isn't that the truth. Teahouses remain open all day, even on windy and rainy days. There are patrons coming from every trade and profession and the teahouses are a natural focal point of thrilling and uncommon news, which makes chatting a true delight. The Sichuanese like to say, "Chat together, pay separately", meaning that strangers feel at ease while talking to each other. This is what Chengdu's teahouse culture is truly about.

**Jiang Yihua:** There are countless teahouses in Chengdu. Apart from the Shunxing Old Teahouse, are there any other famous teahouses?

**Da Meng:** Heming Teahouse at People's Park counts as Chengdu's most populous old teahouse. Patrons pay 30 yuan on average and may stay for half a day while having Bitan Piaoxue tea. Since it is an outdoor teahouse, patrons may get comfortable in tree shades or on lakes. You will find a similar experience at the outdoor teahouses at Wenshu Monastery and Baihuatan Park as well as at the Suiyue Teahouse at Jin River. The Pengzhen Old Teahouse is charming in its historical and marketplace ambience, a lot of amateur photographers go there to collect local cultural material. For the local elderly, this is their favorite place. Whenever there is a market, the place is a sea of teahouse patrons, filled with excitement, as the people are chatting and laughing about everything under the sun over a cup of tea.

**Wen Xiaoxi:** Wow! So many fascinating teahouses, I want to go to them all!

**Jiang Yihua:** I'm also intrigued. Let's go right away!

Part 2  Performance at the Teahouse

**Jiang Yihua:** Da Meng, Mom and Dad are coming to China to see me. They've already been to many of Chengdu's historical sites and scenic spots. Where should I take them to this time?

**Da Meng:** What about a teahouse? Go to a nice one, have some tea and snacks, chat, and you can also play mahjong.

**Wen Xiaoxi:** Great idea! Teahouses are the best places for Chengdu people to chat, receive guests, talk business, work and play mahjong.

**Jiang Yihua:** All right. This time, give them a taste of the Old City's teahouse culture.

**Da Meng:** There are lots of teahouses to choose from: for drama, there is the Shunxing Old Teahouse, for example; for performances of the art of tea, you could go to Chunxi Road's "Shanzhong Old Teahouse"; and there are also the artistic teahouses that are valued by young people, for example the"Hejing Teahouse"and the "Buyuan Shuxiade Courtyard".

**Jiang Yihua:** My parents and I will go to the "Shunxing Old Teahouse" first to experience Sichuan opera and taste some Sichuanese snacks. The service over there is also pretty good. If we still have time, we will also go to the teahouse of tea arts and watch the gongfu tea ceremony.

(Wen Xiaoxi, Da Meng, Jiang Yihua and his parents are in the teahouse)


**Waiter:** We have a drama performance today. You're welcome to watch.

**Jiang Yihua:** The Sichuan drama performed here is extremely popular. Mom, Dad, we'll go watch the drama in just a moment.

**Mom&Dad:** All right, Yihua. Your Chinese has improved quite a bit.

**Wen Xiaoxi:** Yihua fell immediately in love with Chengdu after his arrival. He's giving it all to study Chinese and Chinese culture.

**Dad:** So glad to hear it! I'll go tell Grandma once we're back; she'll be overjoyed.

**Da Meng:** Everybody, have a sit and drink some tea. Yihua, why don't you introduce Sichuan tea; you're also a tea expert now.

**Jiang Yihua:** Dad, you love drinking green tea. I suggest you go with Zhuye Qing. Mom, I recommend having some flowering tea.

**Mom&Dad:** All right!

**Da Meng:** There! Look! The face changing has started!

Part 3  Tea Ceremony Houses

**Wen Xiaoxi:** We've been walking for almost two hours now. I'm feeling a bit exhausted. What about having some gongfu tea and rest for a while?

**Jiang Yihua:** Good idea! The teahouse here offers gongfu tea for groups, and the place itself is nice and cheap. Let's stay a while and have some tea.

(The tea ceremony master starts the gongfu tea ceremony)

**Wen Xiaoxi:** The tea is fragrant, but the waiter poured away the first cup. What a waste, pouring away this magnificent tea!

**Da Meng:** You shouldn't drink the first cup, which is called wash tea (rinsing the leaves) and is a certain step of the gongfu tea ceremony.

**Wen Xiaoxi:** Fine. I have a question. There are so many teas, but their taste doesn't differ too much. Is there any difference at all?

**Da Meng:** There are lots of different teas: black teas, green teas, oolong tea – their effects are not the same. Black tea, for example chuanhong, helps with digestion, relieves fatigue and is good for our gastric flora. Green tea, for example Zhuye Qing, can help against aging and lowers blood fat levels. Oolong is famous for its health and beauty benefits.

**Wen Xiaoxi:** Amazing! I'll have more Sichuan tea then for my health and beauty.

In Sichuan, you can see teahouses everywhere. Statistics show that Chengdu has currently more than 30,000 teahouses in all kinds of styles, be it elegant, simple, traditional, anything that teahouse guests may desire. Sichuan's teahouses emerged early on, have quickly developed and boast a wide range of equipment, are many in number and serve a myriad of purposes; they are something of the very best you can find in the whole country. If you go to Sichuan, to Chengdu, but do not enter a teahouse and have some gaiwan tea, you would definitely miss out. Here, having tea is not about the act of drinking; it is more about enjoying leisure.

(Before, Chengdu's teahouses, small and large, would be filled with patrons from dawn until dusk. On the low end, some stay for two or three hours, whereas others stay all day. Over the course of many years, life has become hurried, but Chengdu's leisurely and comfortable lifestyle has remained unchanged over generations.

Chengdu's teahouses serve a broad variety of purposes. First, they are the best places for chatting. They provide a comfortable environment for chatting for two reasons: a) they open early and close late, have tea and seats, and remain open all day, even on windy and rainy days; b) patrons come from far and near, from every trade and profession, and take their experience to the teahouses, where news comes and goes with the patrons. It is thanks to chatting that the teahouses are growing more and more prosperous. Second, for businesspeople, teahouses serve as an information market. Information is important for business, and so some business people from the same industry make an appointment at the teahouse, where they talk business matters and share  new information over a cup of tea. Third, teahouses  are also good places for friends to come together, for fun or for peace and quiet, teahouses have it all. Last, teahouses are also "everybody's club". People can watch drama, play chess and mahjong, read books and newspapers, and so on.

词 语

| 养 生 yǎngshēng<br>keep in good health | 实 惠 shí huì<br>cheap | 匆 匆 cōng cōng<br>fast |

| qí wén yì shì<br>奇 闻 逸 事 | sth. unheard-of; a thrilling, fantastic story; anecdote | liú chuán<br>流 传 | spread |
|---|---|---|---|
| qiè yì<br>惬 意 | comfortable | gōng xiào<br>功 效 | effect |
| shì jǐng<br>市 井 | marketplace | gāo yǎ<br>高 雅 | elegance |
| pǔ sù<br>朴 素 | simple | huì jí<br>汇 集 | compile |
| xīn wèi<br>欣 慰 | be gratified | yí hàn<br>遗 憾 | a pity |

| xián shì<br>闲 适 | leisurely and comfortable |
|---|---|

| xīng wàng<br>兴 旺 | prosperous |
|---|---|

| wén yì fàn er<br>文 艺 范 儿 | literary style |
|---|---|
| shǔ yī shǔ èr<br>数 一 数 二 | one of the very best |
| tán xiào fēng shēng<br>谈 笑 风 生 | chatting and laughing |

语言点

1. 仅

2. 之

3. 首先……其次……再次……最后……

4. 一……就……

5. 其实

# 思 考

1. 成都茶馆有什么特点？

2. 成都茶馆有哪些功能？

3. "摆龙门阵"是什么意思？

4. 成都有哪些有名的茶馆？它们都有什么特点？

5. 茶艺馆是什么样子的？

# 第五课 〔茶马互市〕
# Lesson 5 【The Tea-Horse Trade】

## （一）中国最早的茶商

① 典 雅　diǎnyǎ
② 购物狂　gòuwùkuáng
③ 穿 越　chuānyuè
④ 遗 址　yízhǐ
⑤ 勤 劳　qínláo

江一华：
今天老师讲的茶马互市太难了，不过挺有意思的。

林 川：
成都是中国最早买卖茶叶的地方，这里的茶叶市场有两千多年历史了。

文小西：
怪不得这里大街小巷都有茶叶店，里面的装修也都很典雅呢。

大 萌：
而且成都的茶叶商人都热情极了，每次去都让我品尝不同的茶叶，喝了不少好茶呢。

文小西：
你也买了不少吧。

大 萌：
我可不是购物狂！你们知道一匹马能换多少茶叶吗？

① 合 作　hézuò
② 瞩 目　zhǔmù
③ 共 赢　gòngyíng
④ 智 慧　zhìhuì

**江一华：**
别开玩笑了，谁会用马换茶叶啊？

**大萌：**
早在唐代，四川茶商就开始用茶叶换藏族的马匹了，而且一换就是几百年呢。

**文小西：**
听起来真有意思，我好想去唐朝看看呀。

**江一华：**
你想穿越到唐朝去？

**大萌：**
穿越肯定是不可能的，不过我们可以去看看茶马古道的遗址。

## （二）茶马古道

**大萌：**
茶马贸易在宋代最兴盛，总管机构"都大茶马司"就在成都。

**江一华：**
看来成都是茶马古道的起点了。

**大** 萌：

对，今天我们要去的是雅安茶马古道。
走，我们去见识见识吧。

**文** 小西：

当时的马帮真辛苦，带着这么重
的茶叶在山路上走。

**江** 一华：

难怪川茶能传遍全世界，都是勤
劳的四川人背出去的。

**大** 萌：

茶马古道又叫古南丝绸之路，以前是贸易
之路和文化交流之路，现在是旅游之路了。

**文** 小西：

新闻里经常看到"一带一路"，
原来和茶马古道也有关系。

**大** 萌：

2017年5月14日在北京举行了"一带
一路"国际高峰论坛。那可是世界瞩目的
一次活动。"一带"是"丝绸之路经济带"，
"一路"是"21世纪海上丝绸之路"，是
中国跟世界上一些国家合作和发展的大工
程。四川的茶马古道就是古代丝绸之路的
一部分，所以曾经的茶马古道现在也是繁
荣发展和合作共赢之路。

（三）山间铃响马帮来

江一华：
　　我看了一部关于马帮的电影！

马兰：
　　茶马古道上的马帮？

文小西：
　　上次去雅安看遗址只觉得他们辛苦，看了电影才知道，他们的勇气和智慧更让人佩服！

马兰：
　　看来我也要去学习一下马帮精神。

江一华：
　　我们一起去看吧，我正好想再看一遍，练练中文听力，感受古老的茶马文化。

马兰：
　　好啊，什么时候有空？如果我们看不懂，还有大萌可以帮我们。

Part 1    China's Earliest Tea Trade

(During break, the students are standing about in knots in the classroom)

**Jiang Yihua:** What the teacher told us about the tea-horse trade today is really difficult to understand. It sounded fascinating, though.

**Lin Chuan:** Chengdu was the first place for tea trading in China. The tea market here has a history of more than 2,000 years.

**Wen Xiaoxi:** No wonder there are tea shops around every corner. Their interiors are also quite elegantly decorated.

**Da Meng:** Chengdu's tea traders are so passionate! Every time I go to their shops, they let me taste different teas. I had so many great teas already!

**Wen Xiaoxi:** Knowing you, you probably bought a lot.

**Da Meng:** Hey, I'm no shopaholic! Do you know how much tea you can get for one horse?

**Jiang Yihua:** Stop joking around; who would exchange a horse for tea?

**Da Meng:** Early on in the Tang Dynasty, Sichuan tea traders started to barter their tea for Tibetan ponies. This practice carried on for hundreds of years.

**Wen Xiaoxi:** You don't say! I'd like to go to the Tang Dynasty and see it for myself.

**Jiang Yihua:** Do you want to travel through time?

**Da Meng:** That's certainly not an option, but what we can do is go to the Tea-Horse Road and have a look.

Part 2  The Tea-Horse Road

(At the Ya'an site of the Tea-Horse Road)

**Da Meng:** The tea-horse trade was at its peak during the Song Dynasty and its main regulatory authority, the "Tea-Horse Trade Affairs Management Department", is located in Chengdu.

**Jiang Yihua:** Looks like Chengdu is the starting point of the Tea-Horse Road.

**Da Meng:** Correct. Today, we're going to the Ya'an site of the Tea-Horse Road and learn something new.

**Wen Xiaoxi:** The caravan of horses sure didn't have it easy at that time, carrying all that heavy tea with them.

**Jiang Yihua:** It's no surprise that Sichuan tea spread throughout the world. It was the diligent Sichuanese who brought tea to the world!

**Da Meng:** The Tea-Horse Road is also called The Southern Silk Road, serving as a route for trade and cultural exchange then and as a route for tourists now.

**Wen Xiaoxi:** You often hear "The Belt and Road" in the news. Turns out The Belt and Road and the Tea-Horse Road share a connection.

**Da Meng:** The Belt and Road Forum for International Cooperation was held in Beijing on May 14th, 2017. The whole world had its eyes on that event. "The Belt" refers to the "Silk Road Economic Belt", while "Road" refers to the "21st Century Maritime Silk Road". The Belt and Road is a large-scale cooperation and development strategy between China and other countries. Sichuan's Tea-Horse Road is part of the ancient silk road, so the once prosperous Tea-Horse Road will today serve again as a route for cooperation and mutual benefits.

Part 3　Caravans with Ring

**Jiang Yihua:** I watched a movie about horse caravans!

**Ma Lan:** Those from the Tea-Horse Road?

**Wen Xiaoxi:** Last time when we were in Ya'an, I thought they had it pretty tough. After I watched the movie, I realized that their courage and wisdom made the traders feel at ease.

**Ma Lan:** Looks like I should learn more about these caravans.

**Jiang Yihua:** Let's go together! I also want them to watch again, improve my listening comprehension and experience the ancient tea-horse culture.

**Ma Lang:** Great! When are you available? If we don't understand something, Da Meng can help us out.

## 词 语

| 购 物 狂 | gòuwùkuáng a person who is crazy about shopping | 瞩 目 | zhǔ mù focus one's attention upon | 合 作 | hé zuò cooperation |

| 典 雅 | (of diction, etc.) refined; elegant |
| diǎn yǎ | |
| 勤 劳 | industrious; hardworking |
| qín láo | |
| 穿 越 | return to ancient time |
| chuān yuè | |

| 遗 址 | site |
| yí zhǐ | |
| 智 慧 | wisdom |
| zhì huì | |
| 共 赢 | win-win |
| gòng yíng | |

## 语言点

1. 怪不得、难怪
2. 可不是

## 思考

1. 茶马互市是什么意思？
2. 四川茶马互市的遗址在哪里？
3. 茶马古道还有什么名字？
4. 茶马古道跟"一带一路"有什么关系？
5. "马帮精神"就是"丝路精神"吗？

# 第六课 〔川茶与"一带一路"〕
# Lesson 6 〔 Sichuan Tea and "The Belt and Road" 〕

① 支付宝　zhīfùbǎo
② 搞　定　gǎodìng
③ 票　选　piàoxuǎn
④ 四大发明　sìdà fāmíng
⑤ 高　铁　gāotiě
⑥ 共享单车　gòngxiǎng dānchē
⑦ 网　购　wǎnggòu
⑧ 剁手族　duòshǒuzú

## （一）礼物

马兰：

下个月就要回国了，我想给亲人和朋友们带些礼物，买什么好呢？

林川：

四川茶叶挺有名的，就带点茶叶好了。竹叶青呀，峨眉雪芽呀，蒙顶甘露什么的，都不错。

马兰：

其实我最想带回家的是支付宝，到哪里都不用带钱包，带着手机就可以搞定一切，太方便了。

江一华：

哈哈。很多同学都这么说，最近外国留学生票选出了新的中国"四大发明"，你们猜是什么。

文小西：

一定有茶道。

江一华：

　茶道也有不少留学生选，但不是前四名，我宣布谜底吧，新的中国"四大发明"是高铁、支付宝、共享单车和网购。

马 兰：

　太有道理了！这些我都想带回国，但是现在只是梦想啦。

大 萌：

　梦想很快就会实现。"一带一路"就是要互联互通，互利共赢，让中国的发展成果也给"一带一路"沿线国家带去好处。目前，中老铁路已经开工建设，印尼的雅万高铁也开工了，中欧班列已经开通，相信很快"一带一路"的沿线国家都能享受到中国的新"四大发明"了。以后海淘网购也会更方便，速度更快，价格更低。

江一华：

　大萌，你还想买，我的房间已经快被你装满了。我看你不仅是购物狂，更是剁手族呢。

## （二）带着川茶去旅行

①茶博士　chábóshì
②绵　延　miányán

**文**小西：

　　嗨！一华，你写什么呢？

**江**一华：

　　我受到了些启发，现在有个很好的想法。

**文**小西：

　　什么好想法，分享一下。

**江**一华：

　　我们之前去了雅安看茶马古道的遗址，后来又了解了"一带一路"，古代中国人带着茶叶走遍了丝绸之路，我也想带着茶叶走一走"一带一路"沿线国家，这趟旅行一定很有意思。

**大**萌：

　　你要改行卖茶叶了？可是现在都是网购了，谁买你的呀？

**江**一华：

　　带茶叶不是做生意，是拍照留念，还有交朋友。你看我们班很多同学都来自"一带一路"国家，我到了他们的家乡，可以拿着茶叶拍照，大家一起喝杯茶，摆摆龙门阵，就像回到了成都的茶馆一样。

**马兰：**

真有意思，你来吧，欢迎你到我家来坐坐。

**大萌：**

嗯。你带我一起去吧。我可是友谊的使者，又是国际大明星，肯定走到哪里都很受欢迎。

**文小西：**

你也得带上我，我可以当茶博士，给大家泡泡茶，聊聊我们的成都生活呀。

**江一华：**

好好好！我们找时间计划一下，准备做"一带一路"的友谊使者吧。

"一带一路"是"丝绸之路经济带"和"21世纪海上丝绸之路"的简称，它从古丝绸之路绵延千年而来。"一带一路"倡议是习近平2013年秋天在哈萨克斯坦和印度尼西亚提出的。"一带一路"以"政策沟通、设施联通、贸易畅通、资金融通、民心相通"为主要内容，像一条神奇的纽带，让中国与世界各国的交往变得绚丽多彩。

Part 1　Gifts

(Ma Lan is returning to her country. She wants to buy some Chinese specialties as gifts)

**Ma Lan:** Next month I'm returning home. I want to buy some presents for my relatives and friends. Anything come to mind?

**Lin Chuan:** Sichuan tea is quite famous, so take some tea with you. Zhuye Qing, Emei Xueya, Mengding Ganlu and so on are all pretty good.

**Ma Lan:** Actually, what I want to take back home the most is Alipay. With just your phone you can settle anything, and there's no need to carry a wallet around with you. It's just so convenient.

**Jiang Yihua:** Haha, right. Many of our peers think the same. Recently, the international students voted for China's new "Four Great Inventions". Can you guess what they are?

**Wen Xiaoxi:** The tea ceremony is definitely among them.

**Jiang Yihua:** The tea ceremony was voted for by many, but it didn't place in the first four ranks. I'm telling you the answer. China's new "Four Great Inventions" are the bullet train, Alipay, bicycle sharing and online shopping.

**Ma Lan:** Well chosen! I want to take all of them back home. Too bad it'll only happen in my dreams.

**Da Meng:** Your dream will become reality very soon. "The Belt and Road" aims for connectedness and mutual benefits by letting the countries along "The Belt and Road" enjoy the fruits of China's development. Currently, construction of both the China-Laos Railway and Indonesia's high-speed rail have started. There are also new train routes between China and Europe. I believe that the countries along "The Belt and Road" will be able to enjoy China's new "Four Great Inventions" rather sooner than later. In the future, buying goods from overseas online will be even more convenient, faster and cheaper.

**Jiang Yihua:** Da Meng, you always like to buy stuff, so much so that our room is almost completely packed. I get it, you're more than a shopaholic, and you're an online shopaholic.

Part 2  Travelling with Tea

**Wen Xiaoxi:** Hi! Yihua, what are you writing there?

**Jiang Yihua:** I had a stroke of inspiration and have come to a conclusion.

**Wen Xiaoxi:** What conclusion? Tell us about it!

**Jiang Yihua:** We've been to the Ya'an site of the Tea-Horse Road and learnt more about "The Belt and Road". Ancient Chinese carried tea to every nook and cranny of the silk road. I too want to carry tea while visiting the countries along "The Belt and Road". I'm sure it'll be a journey worth doing.

**Da Meng:** Do you want to become a tea trader? But now everybody shops online; who would buy your tea?

**Jiang Yihua:** I wouldn't be doing this for business, but for taking pictures and making new friends. You know, a lot of our classmates come from the countries along "The Belt and Road". Once I arrive at their home towns, I would take a photo with the tea. We would have a cup of tea together and chat, just as if we were back in Chengdu's teahouses.

**Ma Lan:** You're really something else! You're welcome to visit me back home.

**Da Meng:** I agree. Take me with you! I'm an ambassador of friendship and also an international superstar. I'm sure I'd be popular everywhere.

**Wen Xiaoxi:** I also want to go! I could be the waitress making tea for everybody, while we'd be talking about our lives in Chengdu.

**Jiang Yihua:** All right! Let's make some time to plan and prepare for our mission of friendship on "The Belt and Road".

"The Belt and Road" stands for "The Silk Road Economic Belt" and "The 21st Century Maritime Silk Road". It is a continuation of the several-thousand-year-old ancient Silk Road. The "Belt and Road Initiative" was proposed by Xi Jinping in Kazakhstan and Indonesia in the autumn of 2013. Its main goal is to promote "policy coordination, infrastructure connectivity, unimpeded trade, financial integration and intercultural communication", like a mystical bond between China and the world, making multilateral relationships more colorful and varied.

## 词语

| 支付宝 zhīfùbǎo Alipay | 沟通 gōutōng communication | 贸易 màoyì trade |

| | |
|---|---|
| gǎo dìng<br>搞 定 — get it | mián yán<br>绵 延 — be continuous |
| wǎng gòu<br>网 购 — online shopping | gāo tiě<br>高 铁 — bullet train |
| chá bó shì<br>茶 博 士 — waiters in an old-time teahouse | duò shǒu zú<br>剁 手 族 — shopaholic |
| piào xuǎn<br>票 选 — vote | zhèng cè<br>政 策 — policy |
| gòu wù kuáng<br>购 物 狂 — shopaholic | shè shī<br>设 施 — facilities |

# 生词

| | |
|---|---|
| lián tōng<br>联 通 | interconnection |
| chàng tōng<br>畅 通 | unimpeded |
| zī jīn<br>资 金 | capital;fund |
| róng tōng<br>融 通 | finance |
| mín xīn<br>民 心 | common aspiration of the people |

| | |
|---|---|
| xiāng tōng<br>相 通 | be interlinked |
| shén qí<br>神 奇 | magical |
| niǔ dài<br>纽 带 | link |
| xuàn lì duō cǎi<br>绚 丽 多 彩 | gorgeous |
| sì dà fā míng<br>四 大 发 明 | four great inventions |

| | |
|---|---|
| yí dài yí lù<br>一 带 一 路 | The Belt and Road Initiative |

# 语言点

1. ……狂
2. ……族

# 思考

1. "一带一路"倡议是谁提出的?

2. 外国留学生回国想带什么?

3. "一带一路"建设可以带来什么好处?

4. 江一华想怎么旅游?

5. 大萌要做什么?

# 第七课 〔古今川茶〕
## Lesson 7 〔Ancient and Modern Sichuan Tea〕

世界上很多国家和地区都种茶、饮茶，但种茶的发源地是中国。在中国，种茶、饮茶最早的地区是四川。

《茶经》上说："茶者，南方之嘉木也，……其巴山峡川有两人合抱者。"陆羽的年代，四川就有双人合抱的大茶树。四川不但种茶树最早，而且高质量的名茶也出现得很早。《华阳国志》上说：汉晋时期，什邡"山出好茶"。四川也是出产茶最多的地方。明末清初，蜀茶产量仍居全国首位，年产量在三千万斤左右。著名文学家苏轼也曾指出："邛、蜀、彭、汉、绵、雅等州……人户以种茶为生。"

现在，四川茶业和茶文化也有了新的发展。为了满足消费者的需要，四川的茶叶品种更多，质量也更优良了。除了传统的名山蒙顶茶、灌县（今都江堰）"青城雪芽"、峨眉茶等名茶外，新品种"川红"也受到国际好评，成为外贸的畅销品种。

① 嘉 木　jiāmù
② 优 良　yōuliáng
③ 外 贸　wàimào
④ 畅 销　chàngxiāo
⑤ 好 评　hǎopíng

A lot of countries and places in the world grow and drink tea, but growing tea is originally a Chinese practice. In China itself, it was the Sichuanese who were the first to grow and drink tea.

*The Classic of Tea* says, "Tea is a magnificent tree growing in the South. In Bashan and the river gorges of Sichuan, there are tea trees growing to such a size that it would take two people hand in hand to embrace their circumference." At Lu Yu's time, Sichuan had trees so big that it would take two people to embrace them! Sichuan was not only the first place to plant tea, but high-quality, famous tea emerged very early on. *The Chronicles of Huayang* say, good tea came out of the mountains of Shifang during the Han and Jin Dynasties. Sichuan is also the place with the highest tea production. In late Ming and early Qing, Sichuan continued to rank first in producing the most tea across the country, with yearly production amounting to about 30 million pounds. The famous writer Su Shi once said, "Be it Qiong, Shu, Peng, Han, Mian or Ya, everyone lives for planting tea."

Today, the Sichuan tea industry and tea culture is going in new directions. In order to satisfy consumer needs, Sichuan offers a larger variety of teas and their quality has even more increased. Apart from traditional, famous teas, such as Mingshan Mengding tea, Guanxian Qingcheng Xueya and Emei tea, a new variety called Chuanhong has also been well received abroad and has sold well on foreign markets.

词 语

好评

| 好 评 | hǎopíng |
| | praise, well received |

畅销

| 畅 销 | chàngxiāo |
| | sell well |

| nián dài | |
| 年 代 | age |
| yōu liáng | |
| 优 良 | excellent |

| jiā mù | |
| 嘉 木 | nice tree |
| wài mào | |
| 外 贸 | foreign trade |

语 言 点

1. "其"的用法　　2. 除了……(以外)，也……

参考文献
[ References ]

[1] 何小竹 . 成都茶馆：一市居民半茶客 [M]. 成都：成都时代出版社，2015:2-139.

[2] 黄世礼 . 川茶文化古今谈 [J]. 四川商业高等专科学校学报，2000(22)：58-61.

[3] 从茶叶了解中国的近代外贸史 [EB/OL].http://bbs.fobshanghai.com/thread-5337527-1-1.html.

[4] 赵银平 . "一带一路"—— 习近平之道 [EB/OL].http://news.xinhuanet.com/politics/2017-05/19/c_129607528.htm.